NATIONAL GALLERY
OF ART
AMERICAN MASTERPIECE
ADDRESS BOOK

The
NATIONAL GALLERY
OF ART
AMERICAN MASTERPIECE
ADDRESS BOOK

With reproductions from the
American Collection of the National Gallery of Art.

Published by
Rutledge Books/Galison

ISBN 0-939456-02-8

Distributed by KAMPMANN & COMPANY

Printed in Japan.

Design by Dana Levy

All illustrations courtesy of
the National Gallery of Art,
Washington, D.C.

Cover illustration:
MISS MARY ELLISON (detail)
Mary Cassatt
Chester Dale Collection

Published by Rutledge Books / Galison
25 West 43rd Street
New York, N.Y. 10036

Welcome to the
NATIONAL GALLERY OF ART
AMERICAN MASTERPIECE ADDRESS BOOK
which includes 40 reproductions from the
Gallery's magnificent American collection.

Selecting these few works from the many
treasures there was difficult. As you view the
collection, which ranges from paintings by
unknown artists of early Colonial times to the
giants of the twentieth century,
you will see why.

We do hope that you enjoy using your
AMERICAN MASTERPIECE ADDRESS BOOK,
that it will remind you of pleasant visits
to the National Gallery, and that it soon will
be time to return.

INDEX TO PAINTINGS

MAHANTANGO VALLEY FARM (detail)
Unknown American Artist
Late 19th century
28 x 35⅜ in.
Gift of Edgar William and Bernice
Chrysler Garbisch

NAME

ADDRESS

PHONE

NAME

ADDRESS

PHONE

NAME

ADDRESS

PHONE

NAME

ADDRESS

PHONE

NAME

ADDRESS

PHONE

NAME

ADDRESS

PHONE

LITTLE GIRL IN WHITE
James McNeill Whistler
c. 1890/1900
14⅛ x 10¼ in.
Gift of Chester Dale

NAME

ADDRESS

PHONE

NAME	NAME
ADDRESS	ADDRESS
PHONE	PHONE

NAME	NAME
ADDRESS	ADDRESS
PHONE	PHONE

NAME	NAME
ADDRESS	ADDRESS
PHONE	PHONE

NAME	NAME
ADDRESS	ADDRESS
PHONE	PHONE

NAME	NAME
ADDRESS	ADDRESS
PHONE	PHONE

NAME	NAME
ADDRESS	ADDRESS
PHONE	PHONE

NAME	NAME
ADDRESS	ADDRESS
PHONE	PHONE

NAME	NAME
ADDRESS	ADDRESS
PHONE	PHONE

NAME

ADDRESS

PHONE

NAME

ADDRESS

PHONE

NAME

ADDRESS

PHONE

NAME

ADDRESS

PHONE

NAME

ADDRESS

PHONE

NAME

ADDRESS

PHONE

NAME

ADDRESS

PHONE

NAME

ADDRESS

PHONE

NAME	NAME
ADDRESS	ADDRESS
PHONE	PHONE

NAME	NAME
ADDRESS	ADDRESS
PHONE	PHONE

NAME	NAME
ADDRESS	ADDRESS
PHONE	PHONE

NAME	NAME
ADDRESS	ADDRESS
PHONE	PHONE

NAME

ADDRESS

PHONE

NAME

ADDRESS

PHONE

NAME

ADDRESS

PHONE

NAME

ADDRESS

PHONE

NAME

ADDRESS

PHONE

NAME

ADDRESS

PHONE

NAME

ADDRESS

PHONE

NAME

ADDRESS

PHONE

NAME	NAME
ADDRESS	ADDRESS
PHONE	PHONE

NAME	NAME
ADDRESS	ADDRESS
PHONE	PHONE

NAME	NAME
ADDRESS	ADDRESS
PHONE	PHONE

NAME	NAME
ADDRESS	ADDRESS
PHONE	PHONE

NAME

ADDRESS

PHONE

NAME

ADDRESS

PHONE

NAME

ADDRESS

PHONE

NAME

ADDRESS

PHONE

NAME

ADDRESS

PHONE

NAME

ADDRESS

PHONE

NAME

ADDRESS

PHONE

LUMBER SCHOONERS AT EVENING ON
    PENOBSCOT BAY (detail)
Fitz Hugh Lane
1860
28 x 40 in.
Andrew W. Mellon Fund and Gift of
    Mr. and Mrs. Francis W. Hatch

B

NAME	NAME
ADDRESS	ADDRESS
PHONE	PHONE

NAME	NAME
ADDRESS	ADDRESS
PHONE	PHONE

NAME	NAME
ADDRESS	ADDRESS
PHONE	PHONE

LADY WITH A LUTE (detail)
Thomas Wilmer Dewing
1886
20 x 15 in.
Gift of Dr. and Mrs. Walter Timme

NAME

ADDRESS

PHONE

NAME	NAME
ADDRESS	ADDRESS
PHONE	PHONE
NAME	NAME
ADDRESS	ADDRESS
PHONE	PHONE
NAME	NAME
ADDRESS	ADDRESS
PHONE	PHONE
NAME	NAME
ADDRESS	ADDRESS
PHONE	PHONE

NAME	NAME
ADDRESS	ADDRESS
PHONE	PHONE

NAME	NAME
ADDRESS	ADDRESS
PHONE	PHONE

NAME	NAME
ADDRESS	ADDRESS
PHONE	PHONE

NAME	NAME
ADDRESS	ADDRESS
PHONE	PHONE

NAME	NAME
ADDRESS	ADDRESS
PHONE	PHONE

NAME	NAME
ADDRESS	ADDRESS
PHONE	PHONE

NAME	NAME
ADDRESS	ADDRESS
PHONE	PHONE

NAME	NAME
ADDRESS	ADDRESS
PHONE	PHONE

NAME

ADDRESS

PHONE

NAME

ADDRESS

PHONE

NAME

ADDRESS

PHONE

NAME

ADDRESS

PHONE

NAME

ADDRESS

PHONE

NAME

ADDRESS

PHONE

NAME

ADDRESS

PHONE

NAME

ADDRESS

PHONE

NAME

ADDRESS

PHONE

NAME

ADDRESS

PHONE

NAME

ADDRESS

PHONE

NAME

ADDRESS

PHONE

NAME

ADDRESS

PHONE

NAME

ADDRESS

PHONE

NAME

ADDRESS

PHONE

NAME

ADDRESS

PHONE

NAME	NAME
ADDRESS	ADDRESS
PHONE	PHONE

NAME	NAME
ADDRESS	ADDRESS
PHONE	PHONE

NAME	NAME
ADDRESS	ADDRESS
PHONE	PHONE

NAME	NAME
ADDRESS	ADDRESS
PHONE	PHONE

NAME

ADDRESS

PHONE

NAME

ADDRESS

PHONE

NAME

ADDRESS

PHONE

NAME

ADDRESS

PHONE

NAME

ADDRESS

PHONE

NAME

ADDRESS

PHONE

NAME

ADDRESS

PHONE

MISS MARY ELLISON (detail)
Mary Cassatt
c. 1880
33½ x 25¾ in.
Chester Dale Collection

C

NAME

ADDRESS

PHONE

NAME

ADDRESS

PHONE

NAME

ADDRESS

PHONE

NAME

ADDRESS

PHONE

NAME

ADDRESS

PHONE

NAME

ADDRESS

PHONE

THE LACKAWANNA VALLEY (detail)
George Inness
1855
33⅞ x 50¼ in.
Gift of Mrs. Huttleston Rogers

NAME

ADDRESS

PHONE

NAME	NAME
ADDRESS	ADDRESS
PHONE	PHONE

NAME	NAME
ADDRESS	ADDRESS
PHONE	PHONE

NAME	NAME
ADDRESS	ADDRESS
PHONE	PHONE

NAME	NAME
ADDRESS	ADDRESS
PHONE	PHONE

NAME	NAME
ADDRESS	ADDRESS
PHONE	PHONE

NAME	NAME
ADDRESS	ADDRESS
PHONE	PHONE

NAME	NAME
ADDRESS	ADDRESS
PHONE	PHONE

NAME	NAME
ADDRESS	ADDRESS
PHONE	PHONE

NAME	NAME
ADDRESS	ADDRESS
PHONE	PHONE

NAME	NAME
ADDRESS	ADDRESS
PHONE	PHONE

NAME	NAME
ADDRESS	ADDRESS
PHONE	PHONE

NAME	NAME
ADDRESS	ADDRESS
PHONE	PHONE

NAME	NAME
ADDRESS	ADDRESS
PHONE	PHONE

NAME	NAME
ADDRESS	ADDRESS
PHONE	PHONE

NAME	NAME
ADDRESS	ADDRESS
PHONE	PHONE

NAME	NAME
ADDRESS	ADDRESS
PHONE	PHONE

NAME	NAME
ADDRESS	ADDRESS
PHONE	PHONE

NAME	NAME
ADDRESS	ADDRESS
PHONE	PHONE

NAME	NAME
ADDRESS	ADDRESS
PHONE	PHONE

NAME	NAME
ADDRESS	ADDRESS
PHONE	PHONE

NAME	NAME
ADDRESS	ADDRESS
PHONE	PHONE

NAME	NAME
ADDRESS	ADDRESS
PHONE	PHONE

NAME	NAME
ADDRESS	ADDRESS
PHONE	PHONE

NAME	NAME
ADDRESS	ADDRESS
PHONE	PHONE

NAME

ADDRESS

PHONE

NAME

ADDRESS

PHONE

NAME

ADDRESS

PHONE

NAME

ADDRESS

PHONE

NAME

ADDRESS

PHONE

NAME

ADDRESS

PHONE

NAME

ADDRESS

PHONE

MRS. JOHN HARRISON AND HER
DAUGHTER MARIA (detail)
Nathaniel Mayhew
c. 1823
30 x 24⅞ in.
Gift of Edgar William and Bernice
Chrysler Garbisch

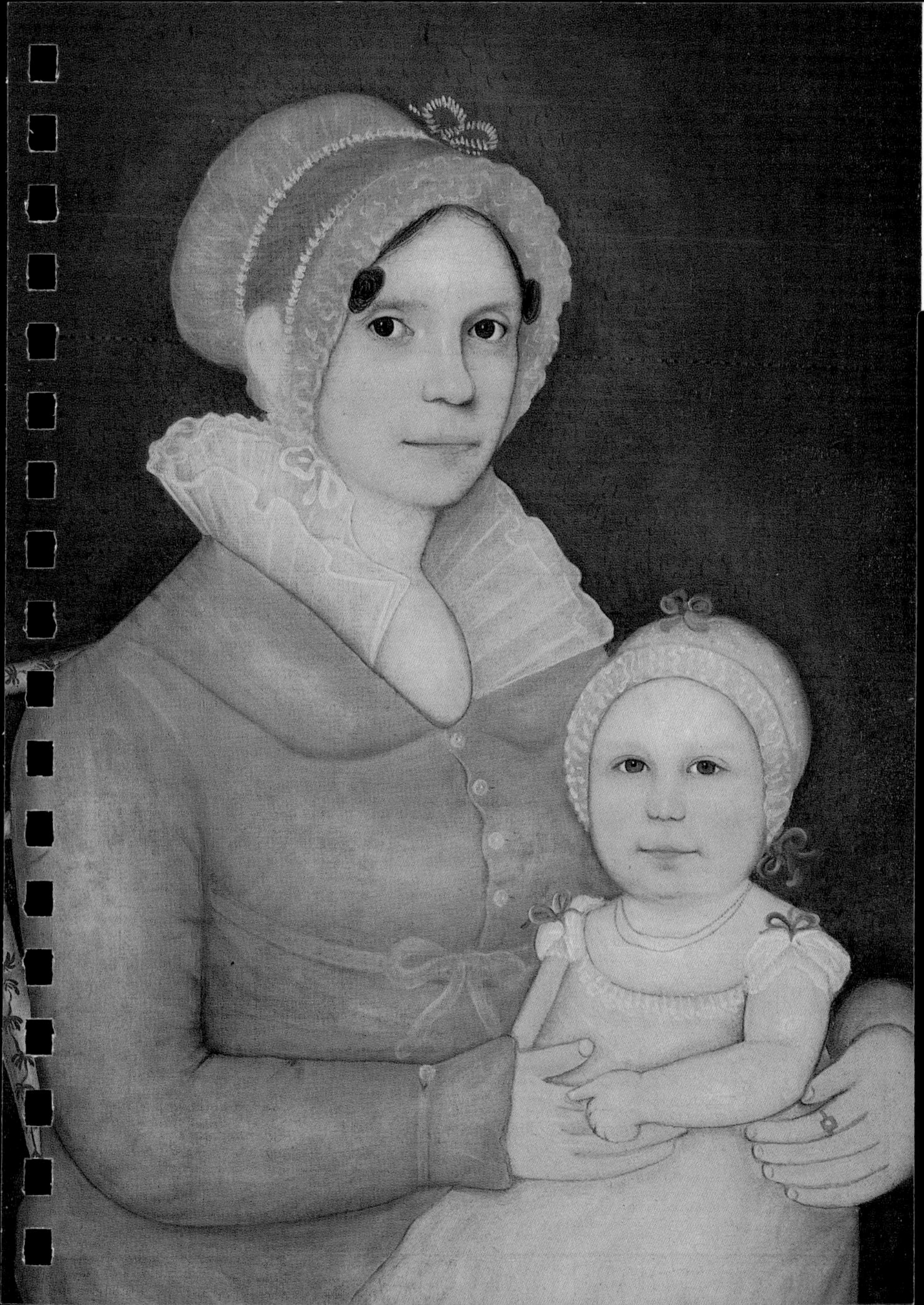

D

NAME

ADDRESS

PHONE

NAME

ADDRESS

PHONE

NAME

ADDRESS

PHONE

NAME

ADDRESS

PHONE

NAME

ADDRESS

PHONE

NAME

ADDRESS

PHONE

AMERICAN WHITE PELICAN
John James Audobon
1836
38⅛ x 25⅝ in.
Mezzotint
Gift of Walter B. James

NAME

ADDRESS

PHONE

NAME	NAME
ADDRESS	ADDRESS
PHONE	PHONE

NAME	NAME
ADDRESS	ADDRESS
PHONE	PHONE

NAME	NAME
ADDRESS	ADDRESS
PHONE	PHONE

NAME	NAME
ADDRESS	ADDRESS
PHONE	PHONE

NAME		NAME
ADDRESS		ADDRESS
PHONE		PHONE
NAME		NAME
ADDRESS		ADDRESS
PHONE		PHONE
NAME		NAME
ADDRESS		ADDRESS
PHONE		PHONE
NAME		NAME
ADDRESS		ADDRESS
PHONE		PHONE

NAME	NAME
ADDRESS	ADDRESS
PHONE	PHONE

NAME	NAME
ADDRESS	ADDRESS
PHONE	PHONE

NAME	NAME
ADDRESS	ADDRESS
PHONE	PHONE

NAME	NAME
ADDRESS	ADDRESS
PHONE	PHONE

NAME	NAME
ADDRESS	ADDRESS
PHONE	PHONE

NAME	NAME
ADDRESS	ADDRESS
PHONE	PHONE

NAME	NAME
ADDRESS	ADDRESS
PHONE	PHONE

NAME	NAME
ADDRESS	ADDRESS
PHONE	PHONE

NAME	NAME
ADDRESS	ADDRESS
PHONE	PHONE

NAME	NAME
ADDRESS	ADDRESS
PHONE	PHONE

NAME	NAME
ADDRESS	ADDRESS
PHONE	PHONE

NAME	NAME
ADDRESS	ADDRESS
PHONE	PHONE

NAME	NAME
ADDRESS	ADDRESS
PHONE	PHONE

NAME	NAME
ADDRESS	ADDRESS
PHONE	PHONE

NAME	NAME
ADDRESS	ADDRESS
PHONE	PHONE

NAME	NAME
ADDRESS	ADDRESS
PHONE	PHONE

NAME

ADDRESS

PHONE

NAME

ADDRESS

PHONE

NAME

ADDRESS

PHONE

NAME

ADDRESS

PHONE

NAME

ADDRESS

PHONE

NAME

ADDRESS

PHONE

NAME

ADDRESS

PHONE

RIO DE JANEIRO BAY (detail)
Martin Johnson Heade
1864
17⅞ x 35⅞ in.
Gift of the Avalon Foundation

EF

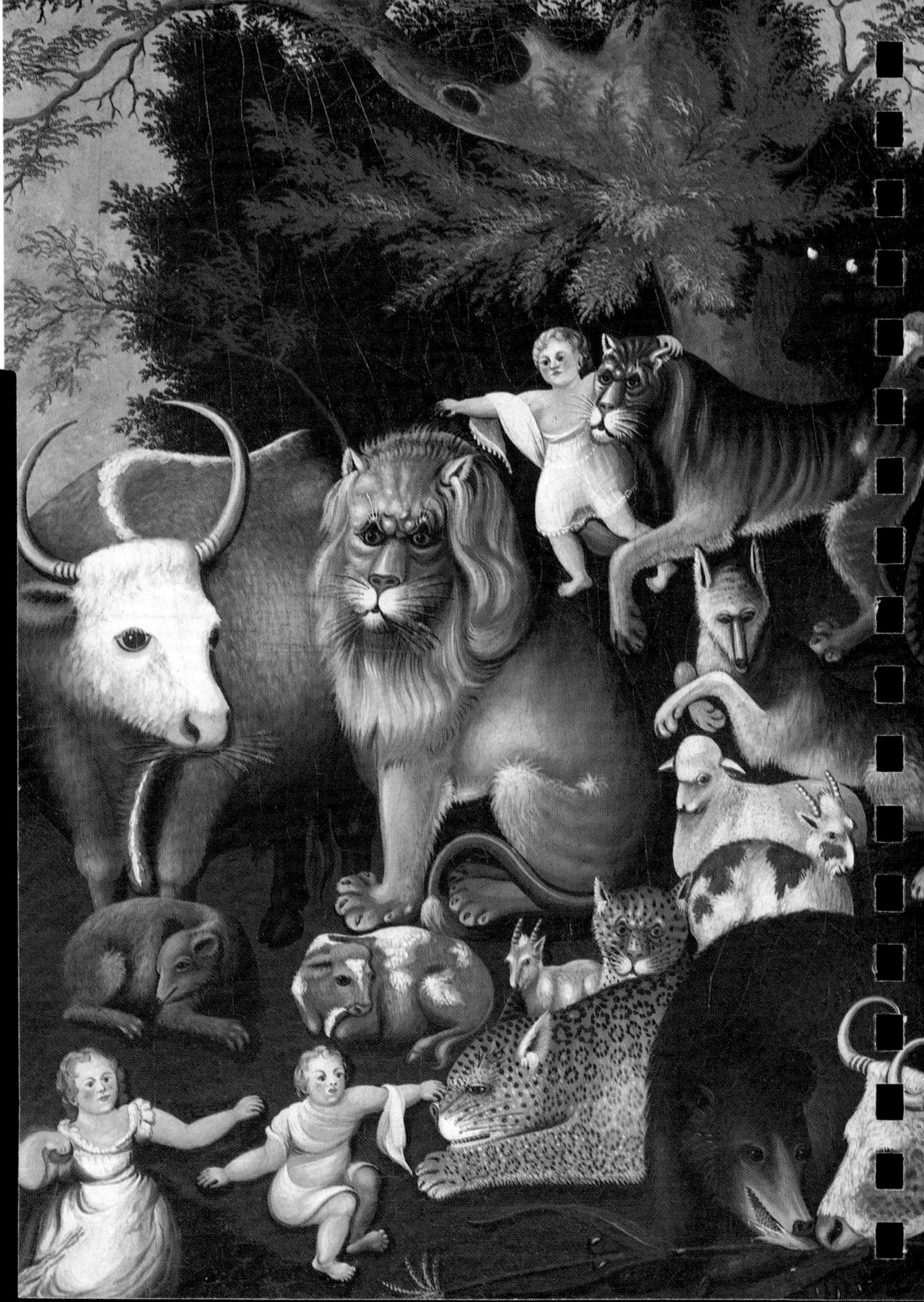

NAME

ADDRESS

PHONE

NAME

ADDRESS

PHONE

NAME

ADDRESS

PHONE

NAME

ADDRESS

PHONE

NAME

ADDRESS

PHONE

NAME

ADDRESS

PHONE

PEACEABLE KINGDOM (detail)
Edward Hicks
c. 1830
30 x 35½ in.
Gift of Edgar William and Bernice
Chrysler Garbisch

NAME

ADDRESS

PHONE

NAME	NAME
ADDRESS	ADDRESS
PHONE	PHONE
NAME	NAME
ADDRESS	ADDRESS
PHONE	PHONE
NAME	NAME
ADDRESS	ADDRESS
PHONE	PHONE
NAME	NAME
ADDRESS	ADDRESS
PHONE	PHONE

NAME

ADDRESS

PHONE

NAME

ADDRESS

PHONE

NAME

ADDRESS

PHONE

NAME

ADDRESS

PHONE

NAME

ADDRESS

PHONE

NAME

ADDRESS

PHONE

NAME

ADDRESS

PHONE

NAME

ADDRESS

PHONE

NAME	NAME
ADDRESS	ADDRESS
PHONE	PHONE

NAME	NAME
ADDRESS	ADDRESS
PHONE	PHONE

NAME	NAME
ADDRESS	ADDRESS
PHONE	PHONE

NAME	NAME
ADDRESS	ADDRESS
PHONE	PHONE

NAME	NAME
ADDRESS	ADDRESS
PHONE	PHONE

NAME	NAME
ADDRESS	ADDRESS
PHONE	PHONE

NAME	NAME
ADDRESS	ADDRESS
PHONE	PHONE

NAME	NAME
ADDRESS	ADDRESS
PHONE	PHONE

NAME

ADDRESS

PHONE

NAME

ADDRESS

PHONE

NAME

ADDRESS

PHONE

NAME

ADDRESS

PHONE

NAME

ADDRESS

PHONE

NAME

ADDRESS

PHONE

NAME

ADDRESS

PHONE

NAME

ADDRESS

PHONE

NAME	NAME
ADDRESS	ADDRESS
PHONE	PHONE
NAME	NAME
ADDRESS	ADDRESS
PHONE	PHONE
NAME	NAME
ADDRESS	ADDRESS
PHONE	PHONE
NAME	NAME
ADDRESS	ADDRESS
PHONE	PHONE

NAME

ADDRESS

PHONE

NAME

ADDRESS

PHONE

NAME

ADDRESS

PHONE

NAME

ADDRESS

PHONE

NAME

ADDRESS

PHONE

NAME

ADDRESS

PHONE

NAME

ADDRESS

PHONE

A FRIENDLY CALL (detail)
William Merritt Chase
1895
30⅛ x 48¼ in.
Gift of Chester Dale

G

NAME

ADDRESS

PHONE

NAME

ADDRESS

PHONE

NAME

ADDRESS

PHONE

NAME

ADDRESS

PHONE

NAME

ADDRESS

PHONE

NAME

ADDRESS

PHONE

CHRYSANTHEMUMS (detail)
William Merritt Chase
c. 1878
26⅞ x 44¾ in.
Gift of Chester Dale

NAME

ADDRESS

PHONE

NAME

ADDRESS

PHONE

NAME

ADDRESS

PHONE

NAME

ADDRESS

PHONE

NAME

ADDRESS

PHONE

NAME

ADDRESS

PHONE

NAME

ADDRESS

PHONE

NAME

ADDRESS

PHONE

NAME

ADDRESS

PHONE

NAME	NAME
ADDRESS	ADDRESS
PHONE	PHONE
NAME	NAME
ADDRESS	ADDRESS
PHONE	PHONE
NAME	NAME
ADDRESS	ADDRESS
PHONE	PHONE
NAME	NAME
ADDRESS	ADDRESS
PHONE	PHONE

NAME _____

ADDRESS _____

_____

_____

PHONE _____

NAME _____

ADDRESS _____

_____

_____

PHONE _____

NAME _____

ADDRESS _____

_____

_____

PHONE _____

NAME _____

ADDRESS _____

_____

_____

PHONE _____

NAME _____

ADDRESS _____

_____

_____

PHONE _____

NAME _____

ADDRESS _____

_____

_____

PHONE _____

NAME _____

ADDRESS _____

_____

_____

PHONE _____

NAME _____

ADDRESS _____

_____

_____

PHONE _____

NAME	NAME
ADDRESS	ADDRESS
PHONE	PHONE

NAME	NAME
ADDRESS	ADDRESS
PHONE	PHONE

NAME	NAME
ADDRESS	ADDRESS
PHONE	PHONE

NAME	NAME
ADDRESS	ADDRESS
PHONE	PHONE

NAME	NAME
ADDRESS	ADDRESS
PHONE	PHONE
NAME	NAME
ADDRESS	ADDRESS
PHONE	PHONE
NAME	NAME
ADDRESS	ADDRESS
PHONE	PHONE
NAME	NAME
ADDRESS	ADDRESS
PHONE	PHONE

NAME	NAME
ADDRESS	ADDRESS
PHONE	PHONE

NAME	NAME
ADDRESS	ADDRESS
PHONE	PHONE

NAME	NAME
ADDRESS	ADDRESS
PHONE	PHONE

NAME	NAME
ADDRESS	ADDRESS
PHONE	PHONE

NAME _____

ADDRESS _____

_____

_____

PHONE _____

NAME _____

ADDRESS _____

_____

_____

PHONE _____

NAME _____

ADDRESS _____

_____

_____

PHONE _____

NAME _____

ADDRESS _____

_____

_____

PHONE _____

NAME _____

ADDRESS _____

_____

_____

PHONE _____

NAME _____

ADDRESS _____

_____

_____

PHONE _____

NAME _____

ADDRESS _____

_____

_____

_____

PHONE _____

MISS DENISON OF STONINGTON,
CONNECTICUT
Unknown American Artist
c. 1785
34½ x 27⅛ in.
Gift of Edgar William and Bernice
Chrysler Garbisch

NAME	NAME
ADDRESS	ADDRESS
PHONE	PHONE

NAME	NAME
ADDRESS	ADDRESS
PHONE	PHONE

NAME	NAME
ADDRESS	ADDRESS
PHONE	PHONE

THE LETTER
Mary Cassatt
1891
347 x 225 mm
Rosenwald Collection

NAME

ADDRESS

PHONE

NAME	NAME
ADDRESS	ADDRESS
PHONE	PHONE

NAME	NAME
ADDRESS	ADDRESS
PHONE	PHONE

NAME	NAME
ADDRESS	ADDRESS
PHONE	PHONE

NAME	NAME
ADDRESS	ADDRESS
PHONE	PHONE

NAME _____

ADDRESS _____

_____

_____

PHONE _____

NAME _____

ADDRESS _____

_____

_____

PHONE _____

NAME _____

ADDRESS _____

_____

_____

PHONE _____

NAME _____

ADDRESS _____

_____

_____

PHONE _____

NAME _____

ADDRESS _____

_____

_____

PHONE _____

NAME _____

ADDRESS _____

_____

_____

PHONE _____

NAME _____

ADDRESS _____

_____

_____

PHONE _____

NAME _____

ADDRESS _____

_____

_____

PHONE _____

NAME

ADDRESS

PHONE

NAME

ADDRESS

PHONE

NAME

ADDRESS

PHONE

NAME

ADDRESS

PHONE

NAME

ADDRESS

PHONE

NAME

ADDRESS

PHONE

NAME

ADDRESS

PHONE

NAME

ADDRESS

PHONE

NAME	NAME
ADDRESS	ADDRESS
PHONE	PHONE

NAME	NAME
ADDRESS	ADDRESS
PHONE	PHONE

NAME	NAME
ADDRESS	ADDRESS
PHONE	PHONE

NAME	NAME
ADDRESS	ADDRESS
PHONE	PHONE

NAME

ADDRESS

PHONE

NAME

ADDRESS

PHONE

NAME

ADDRESS

PHONE

NAME

ADDRESS

PHONE

NAME

ADDRESS

PHONE

NAME

ADDRESS

PHONE

NAME

ADDRESS

PHONE

NAME

ADDRESS

PHONE

NAME	NAME
ADDRESS	ADDRESS
PHONE	PHONE

NAME	NAME
ADDRESS	ADDRESS
PHONE	PHONE

NAME	NAME
ADDRESS	ADDRESS
PHONE	PHONE

NAME	NAME
ADDRESS	ADDRESS
PHONE	PHONE

NAME

ADDRESS

PHONE

NAME

ADDRESS

PHONE

NAME

ADDRESS

PHONE

NAME

ADDRESS

PHONE

NAME

ADDRESS

PHONE

NAME

ADDRESS

PHONE

NAME

ADDRESS

PHONE

GENERAL GEORGE WASHINGTON
ON A WHITE CHARGER
Unknown American Artist
First half of the 19th century
38⅛ x 29⅜ in.
Gift of Edgar William and Bernice
Chrysler Garbisch

NAME

ADDRESS

PHONE

NAME

ADDRESS

PHONE

NAME

ADDRESS

PHONE

NAME

ADDRESS

PHONE

NAME

ADDRESS

PHONE

NAME

ADDRESS

PHONE

THE RAGAN SISTERS (detail)
Jacob Eichholtz
c. 1820
59 x 43 in.
Gift of Mrs. Cooper R. Drewry

NAME

ADDRESS

PHONE

NAME

ADDRESS

PHONE

NAME

ADDRESS

PHONE

NAME

ADDRESS

PHONE

NAME

ADDRESS

PHONE

NAME

ADDRESS

PHONE

NAME

ADDRESS

PHONE

NAME

ADDRESS

PHONE

NAME

ADDRESS

PHONE

NAME	NAME
ADDRESS	ADDRESS
PHONE	PHONE

NAME	NAME
ADDRESS	ADDRESS
PHONE	PHONE

NAME	NAME
ADDRESS	ADDRESS
PHONE	PHONE

NAME	NAME
ADDRESS	ADDRESS
PHONE	PHONE

NAME	NAME
ADDRESS	ADDRESS
PHONE	PHONE

NAME	NAME
ADDRESS	ADDRESS
PHONE	PHONE

NAME	NAME
ADDRESS	ADDRESS
PHONE	PHONE

NAME	NAME
ADDRESS	ADDRESS
PHONE	PHONE

NAME _____

ADDRESS _____

_____

_____

PHONE _____

NAME _____

ADDRESS _____

_____

_____

PHONE _____

NAME _____

ADDRESS _____

_____

_____

PHONE _____

NAME _____

ADDRESS _____

_____

_____

PHONE _____

NAME _____

ADDRESS _____

_____

_____

PHONE _____

NAME _____

ADDRESS _____

_____

_____

PHONE _____

NAME _____

ADDRESS _____

_____

_____

PHONE _____

NAME _____

ADDRESS _____

_____

_____

PHONE _____

NAME	NAME
ADDRESS	ADDRESS
PHONE	PHONE

NAME	NAME
ADDRESS	ADDRESS
PHONE	PHONE

NAME	NAME
ADDRESS	ADDRESS
PHONE	PHONE

NAME	NAME
ADDRESS	ADDRESS
PHONE	PHONE

NAME	NAME
ADDRESS	ADDRESS
PHONE	PHONE

NAME	NAME
ADDRESS	ADDRESS
PHONE	PHONE

NAME	NAME
ADDRESS	ADDRESS
PHONE	PHONE

NAME	NAME
ADDRESS	ADDRESS
PHONE	PHONE

NAME _____

ADDRESS _____

_____

_____

PHONE _____

NAME _____

ADDRESS _____

_____

_____

PHONE _____

NAME _____

ADDRESS _____

_____

_____

PHONE _____

NAME _____

ADDRESS _____

_____

_____

PHONE _____

NAME _____

ADDRESS _____

_____

_____

PHONE _____

NAME _____

ADDRESS _____

_____

_____

PHONE _____

NAME _____

ADDRESS _____

_____

_____

PHONE _____

THE OLD VIOLIN
John Frederick Peto
c. 1890
30⅜ x 22⅞ in.
Gift of the Avalon Foundation

K

NAME

ADDRESS

PHONE

NAME

ADDRESS

PHONE

NAME

ADDRESS

PHONE

NAME

ADDRESS

PHONE

NAME

ADDRESS

PHONE

NAME

ADDRESS

PHONE

THE CORNELL FARM (detail)
Edward Hicks
1848
36¾ x 49 in.
Gift of Edgar William and Bernice
Chrysler Garbisch

NAME

ADDRESS

PHONE

NAME	NAME
ADDRESS	ADDRESS
PHONE	PHONE
NAME	NAME
ADDRESS	ADDRESS
PHONE	PHONE
NAME	NAME
ADDRESS	ADDRESS
PHONE	PHONE
NAME	NAME
ADDRESS	ADDRESS
PHONE	PHONE

NAME _____

ADDRESS _____

_____

_____

PHONE _____

NAME _____

ADDRESS _____

_____

_____

PHONE _____

NAME _____

ADDRESS _____

_____

_____

PHONE _____

NAME _____

ADDRESS _____

_____

_____

PHONE _____

NAME _____

ADDRESS _____

_____

_____

PHONE _____

NAME _____

ADDRESS _____

_____

_____

PHONE _____

NAME _____

ADDRESS _____

_____

_____

PHONE _____

NAME _____

ADDRESS _____

_____

_____

PHONE _____

NAME

ADDRESS

PHONE

NAME

ADDRESS

PHONE

NAME

ADDRESS

PHONE

NAME

ADDRESS

PHONE

NAME

ADDRESS

PHONE

NAME

ADDRESS

PHONE

NAME

ADDRESS

PHONE

NAME

ADDRESS

PHONE

NAME

ADDRESS

PHONE

NAME

ADDRESS

PHONE

NAME

ADDRESS

PHONE

NAME

ADDRESS

PHONE

NAME

ADDRESS

PHONE

NAME

ADDRESS

PHONE

NAME

ADDRESS

PHONE

NAME

ADDRESS

PHONE

NAME	NAME
ADDRESS	ADDRESS
PHONE	PHONE

NAME	NAME
ADDRESS	ADDRESS
PHONE	PHONE

NAME	NAME
ADDRESS	ADDRESS
PHONE	PHONE

NAME	NAME
ADDRESS	ADDRESS
PHONE	PHONE

NAME	NAME
ADDRESS	ADDRESS
PHONE	PHONE

NAME	NAME
ADDRESS	ADDRESS
PHONE	PHONE

NAME	NAME
ADDRESS	ADDRESS
PHONE	PHONE

NAME	NAME
ADDRESS	ADDRESS
PHONE	PHONE

NAME

ADDRESS

PHONE

NAME

ADDRESS

PHONE

NAME

ADDRESS

PHONE

NAME

ADDRESS

PHONE

NAME

ADDRESS

PHONE

NAME

ADDRESS

PHONE

NAME

ADDRESS

PHONE

REPOSE (detail)
John Singer Sargent
1911
$25\frac{1}{8}$ x 30 in.
Gift of Curt H. Reisinger

L

NAME

ADDRESS

PHONE

NAME

ADDRESS

PHONE

NAME

ADDRESS

PHONE

NAME

ADDRESS

PHONE

NAME

ADDRESS

PHONE

NAME

ADDRESS

PHONE

THE POLITICIANS (detail)
Guy Pène Du Bois
c. 1912
16⅛ x 12⅛ in.
Gift of Chester Dale

NAME

ADDRESS

PHONE

NAME	NAME
ADDRESS	ADDRESS
PHONE	PHONE

NAME	NAME
ADDRESS	ADDRESS
PHONE	PHONE

NAME	NAME
ADDRESS	ADDRESS
PHONE	PHONE

NAME	NAME
ADDRESS	ADDRESS
PHONE	PHONE

NAME	NAME
ADDRESS	ADDRESS
PHONE	PHONE

NAME	NAME
ADDRESS	ADDRESS
PHONE	PHONE

NAME	NAME
ADDRESS	ADDRESS
PHONE	PHONE

NAME	NAME
ADDRESS	ADDRESS
PHONE	PHONE

NAME	NAME
ADDRESS	ADDRESS
PHONE	PHONE
NAME	NAME
ADDRESS	ADDRESS
PHONE	PHONE
NAME	NAME
ADDRESS	ADDRESS
PHONE	PHONE
NAME	NAME
ADDRESS	ADDRESS
PHONE	PHONE

NAME	NAME
ADDRESS	ADDRESS
PHONE	PHONE

NAME	NAME
ADDRESS	ADDRESS
PHONE	PHONE

NAME	NAME
ADDRESS	ADDRESS
PHONE	PHONE

NAME	NAME
ADDRESS	ADDRESS
PHONE	PHONE

NAME	NAME
ADDRESS	ADDRESS
PHONE	PHONE

NAME	NAME
ADDRESS	ADDRESS
PHONE	PHONE

NAME	NAME
ADDRESS	ADDRESS
PHONE	PHONE

NAME	NAME
ADDRESS	ADDRESS
PHONE	PHONE

NAME	NAME
ADDRESS	ADDRESS
PHONE	PHONE

NAME	NAME
ADDRESS	ADDRESS
PHONE	PHONE

NAME	NAME
ADDRESS	ADDRESS
PHONE	PHONE

NAME	NAME
ADDRESS	ADDRESS
PHONE	PHONE

NAME

ADDRESS

PHONE

NAME

ADDRESS

PHONE

NAME

ADDRESS

PHONE

NAME

ADDRESS

PHONE

NAME

ADDRESS

PHONE

NAME

ADDRESS

PHONE

NAME

ADDRESS

PHONE

THE ARTIST AND HIS MOTHER (det.)
Arshile Gorky
c. 1929–c. 1930
60 x 50 in.
Ailsa Mellon Bruce Fund

M

NAME

ADDRESS

PHONE

NAME

ADDRESS

PHONE

NAME

ADDRESS

PHONE

NAME

ADDRESS

PHONE

NAME

ADDRESS

PHONE

NAME

ADDRESS

PHONE

THE NOTCH OF THE WHITE
MOUNTAINS (detail)
Thomas Cole
1839
40 x 61½ in.
Andrew W. Mellon Fund

NAME

ADDRESS

PHONE

NAME	NAME
ADDRESS	ADDRESS
PHONE	PHONE
NAME	NAME
ADDRESS	ADDRESS
PHONE	PHONE
NAME	NAME
ADDRESS	ADDRESS
PHONE	PHONE
NAME	NAME
ADDRESS	ADDRESS
PHONE	PHONE

NAME

ADDRESS

PHONE

NAME

ADDRESS

PHONE

NAME

ADDRESS

PHONE

NAME

ADDRESS

PHONE

NAME

ADDRESS

PHONE

NAME

ADDRESS

PHONE

NAME

ADDRESS

PHONE

NAME

ADDRESS

PHONE

NAME

ADDRESS

PHONE

NAME

ADDRESS

PHONE

NAME

ADDRESS

PHONE

NAME

ADDRESS

PHONE

NAME

ADDRESS

PHONE

NAME

ADDRESS

PHONE

NAME

ADDRESS

PHONE

NAME

ADDRESS

PHONE

NAME	NAME
ADDRESS	ADDRESS
PHONE	PHONE

NAME	NAME
ADDRESS	ADDRESS
PHONE	PHONE

NAME	NAME
ADDRESS	ADDRESS
PHONE	PHONE

NAME	NAME
ADDRESS	ADDRESS
PHONE	PHONE

NAME

ADDRESS

PHONE

NAME

ADDRESS

PHONE

NAME

ADDRESS

PHONE

NAME

ADDRESS

PHONE

NAME

ADDRESS

PHONE

NAME

ADDRESS

PHONE

NAME

ADDRESS

PHONE

NAME

ADDRESS

PHONE

NAME	NAME
ADDRESS	ADDRESS
PHONE	PHONE

NAME	NAME
ADDRESS	ADDRESS
PHONE	PHONE

NAME	NAME
ADDRESS	ADDRESS
PHONE	PHONE

NAME	NAME
ADDRESS	ADDRESS
PHONE	PHONE

NAME

ADDRESS

PHONE

NAME

ADDRESS

PHONE

NAME

ADDRESS

PHONE

NAME

ADDRESS

PHONE

NAME

ADDRESS

PHONE

NAME

ADDRESS

PHONE

NAME

ADDRESS

PHONE

PORTRAIT OF FLORENCE DAVEY
George Bellows
1914
38 x 30 in.
Gift of Florence S. McCormack

N

NAME

ADDRESS

PHONE

NAME

ADDRESS

PHONE

NAME

ADDRESS

PHONE

THE SEINE (detail)
Henry O. Tanner
1902
9 x 13 in.
Gift of the Avalon Foundation

NAME

ADDRESS

PHONE

NAME

ADDRESS

PHONE

NAME

ADDRESS

PHONE

NAME

ADDRESS

PHONE

NAME

ADDRESS

PHONE

NAME

ADDRESS

PHONE

NAME

ADDRESS

PHONE

NAME

ADDRESS

PHONE

NAME

ADDRESS

PHONE

NAME

ADDRESS

PHONE

NAME

ADDRESS

PHONE

NAME

ADDRESS

PHONE

NAME	NAME
ADDRESS	ADDRESS
PHONE	PHONE

NAME	NAME
ADDRESS	ADDRESS
PHONE	PHONE

NAME	NAME
ADDRESS	ADDRESS
PHONE	PHONE

NAME	NAME
ADDRESS	ADDRESS
PHONE	PHONE

NAME

ADDRESS

PHONE

NAME

ADDRESS

PHONE

NAME

ADDRESS

PHONE

NAME

ADDRESS

PHONE

NAME

ADDRESS

PHONE

NAME

ADDRESS

PHONE

NAME

ADDRESS

PHONE

NAME

ADDRESS

PHONE

NAME	NAME
ADDRESS	ADDRESS
PHONE	PHONE

NAME	NAME
ADDRESS	ADDRESS
PHONE	PHONE

NAME	NAME
ADDRESS	ADDRESS
PHONE	PHONE

NAME	NAME
ADDRESS	ADDRESS
PHONE	PHONE

NAME

ADDRESS

PHONE

NAME

ADDRESS

PHONE

NAME

ADDRESS

PHONE

NAME

ADDRESS

PHONE

NAME

ADDRESS

PHONE

NAME

ADDRESS

PHONE

NAME

ADDRESS

PHONE

NAME

ADDRESS

PHONE

NAME _____

ADDRESS _____

_____

_____

PHONE _____

NAME _____

ADDRESS _____

_____

_____

PHONE _____

NAME _____

ADDRESS _____

_____

_____

PHONE _____

NAME _____

ADDRESS _____

_____

_____

PHONE _____

NAME _____

ADDRESS _____

_____

_____

PHONE _____

NAME _____

ADDRESS _____

_____

_____

PHONE _____

NAME _____

ADDRESS _____

_____

_____

PHONE _____

NAME _____

ADDRESS _____

_____

_____

PHONE _____

NAME

ADDRESS

PHONE

NAME

ADDRESS

PHONE

NAME

ADDRESS

PHONE

NAME

ADDRESS

PHONE

NAME

ADDRESS

PHONE

NAME

ADDRESS

PHONE

NAME

ADDRESS

PHONE

THE WESTWOOD CHILDREN (detail)
Joshua Johnson
c. 1807
41⅛ x 46 in.
Gift of Edgar William and Bernice
Chrysler Garbisch

O

NAME _____

ADDRESS _____

_____

_____

PHONE _____

NAME _____

ADDRESS _____

_____

_____

PHONE _____

NAME _____

ADDRESS _____

_____

_____

PHONE _____

THE BASHFUL COUSIN (detail)
Francis William Edmonds
c. 1842
25 x 30 in.
Gift of Frederick Sturges, Jr.

NAME _____

ADDRESS _____

_____

_____

PHONE _____

NAME _____

ADDRESS _____

_____

_____

PHONE _____

NAME _____

ADDRESS _____

_____

_____

PHONE _____

NAME _____

ADDRESS _____

_____

_____

PHONE _____

NAME

ADDRESS

PHONE

NAME

ADDRESS

PHONE

NAME

ADDRESS

PHONE

NAME

ADDRESS

PHONE

NAME

ADDRESS

PHONE

NAME

ADDRESS

PHONE

NAME

ADDRESS

PHONE

NAME

ADDRESS

PHONE

NAME

ADDRESS

PHONE

NAME

ADDRESS

PHONE

NAME

ADDRESS

PHONE

NAME

ADDRESS

PHONE

NAME

ADDRESS

PHONE

NAME

ADDRESS

PHONE

NAME

ADDRESS

PHONE

NAME

ADDRESS

PHONE

NAME

ADDRESS

PHONE

NAME

ADDRESS

PHONE

NAME

ADDRESS

PHONE

NAME

ADDRESS

PHONE

NAME

ADDRESS

PHONE

NAME

ADDRESS

PHONE

NAME

ADDRESS

PHONE

NAME

ADDRESS

PHONE

NAME	NAME
ADDRESS	ADDRESS
PHONE	PHONE

NAME	NAME
ADDRESS	ADDRESS
PHONE	PHONE

NAME	NAME
ADDRESS	ADDRESS
PHONE	PHONE

NAME	NAME
ADDRESS	ADDRESS
PHONE	PHONE

NAME

ADDRESS

PHONE

NAME

ADDRESS

PHONE

NAME

ADDRESS

PHONE

NAME

ADDRESS

PHONE

NAME

ADDRESS

PHONE

NAME

ADDRESS

PHONE

NAME

ADDRESS

PHONE

NAME

ADDRESS

PHONE

NAME	NAME
ADDRESS	ADDRESS
PHONE	PHONE

NAME	NAME
ADDRESS	ADDRESS
PHONE	PHONE

NAME	NAME
ADDRESS	ADDRESS
PHONE	PHONE

NAME	NAME
ADDRESS	ADDRESS
PHONE	PHONE

NAME

ADDRESS

PHONE

NAME

ADDRESS

PHONE

NAME

ADDRESS

PHONE

NAME

ADDRESS

PHONE

NAME

ADDRESS

PHONE

NAME

ADDRESS

PHONE

NAME

ADDRESS

PHONE

GEESE IN FLIGHT (detail)
Leila T. Bauman
c. 1870
20¼ x 26¼ in.
Gift of Edgar William and Bernice
Chrysler Garbisch

P

P

NAME

ADDRESS

PHONE

NAME

ADDRESS

PHONE

NAME

ADDRESS

PHONE

NAME

ADDRESS

PHONE

NAME

ADDRESS

PHONE

NAME

ADDRESS

PHONE

CHILDREN PLAYING ON THE BEACH
Mary Cassatt
1884
38⅜ x 29¼ in.
Ailsa Mellon Bruce Collection

NAME

ADDRESS

PHONE

NAME	NAME
ADDRESS	ADDRESS
PHONE	PHONE
NAME	NAME
ADDRESS	ADDRESS
PHONE	PHONE
NAME	NAME
ADDRESS	ADDRESS
PHONE	PHONE
NAME	NAME
ADDRESS	ADDRESS
PHONE	PHONE

NAME	NAME
ADDRESS	ADDRESS
PHONE	PHONE
NAME	NAME
ADDRESS	ADDRESS
PHONE	PHONE
NAME	NAME
ADDRESS	ADDRESS
PHONE	PHONE
NAME	NAME
ADDRESS	ADDRESS
PHONE	PHONE

NAME

ADDRESS

PHONE

NAME

ADDRESS

PHONE

NAME

ADDRESS

PHONE

NAME

ADDRESS

PHONE

NAME

ADDRESS

PHONE

NAME

ADDRESS

PHONE

NAME

ADDRESS

PHONE

NAME

ADDRESS

PHONE

NAME	NAME
ADDRESS	ADDRESS
PHONE	PHONE

NAME	NAME
ADDRESS	ADDRESS
PHONE	PHONE

NAME	NAME
ADDRESS	ADDRESS
PHONE	PHONE

NAME	NAME
ADDRESS	ADDRESS
PHONE	PHONE

NAME	NAME
ADDRESS	ADDRESS
PHONE	PHONE

NAME	NAME
ADDRESS	ADDRESS
PHONE	PHONE

NAME	NAME
ADDRESS	ADDRESS
PHONE	PHONE

NAME	NAME
ADDRESS	ADDRESS
PHONE	PHONE

NAME	NAME
ADDRESS	ADDRESS
PHONE	PHONE

NAME	NAME
ADDRESS	ADDRESS
PHONE	PHONE

NAME	NAME
ADDRESS	ADDRESS
PHONE	PHONE

NAME	NAME
ADDRESS	ADDRESS
PHONE	PHONE

NAME

ADDRESS

PHONE

NAME

ADDRESS

PHONE

NAME

ADDRESS

PHONE

NAME

ADDRESS

PHONE

NAME

ADDRESS

PHONE

NAME

ADDRESS

PHONE

NAME

ADDRESS

PHONE

LIBERTY
Unknown American Artist
Early 19th century
29⅞ x 20 in.
Gift of Edgar William and Bernice
Chrysler Garbisch

QR

NAME	NAME
ADDRESS	ADDRESS
PHONE	PHONE

NAME	NAME
ADDRESS	ADDRESS
PHONE	PHONE

NAME	NAME
ADDRESS	ADDRESS
PHONE	PHONE

GIRL CARRYING A BASKET (detail)
Winslow Homer
1882
371 x 553 mm
Gift of Ruth K. Henschel in memory
of her husband, Charles R. Henschel

NAME

ADDRESS

PHONE

NAME

ADDRESS

PHONE

NAME

ADDRESS

PHONE

NAME

ADDRESS

PHONE

NAME

ADDRESS

PHONE

NAME

ADDRESS

PHONE

NAME

ADDRESS

PHONE

NAME

ADDRESS

PHONE

NAME

ADDRESS

PHONE

NAME	NAME
ADDRESS	ADDRESS
PHONE	PHONE

NAME	NAME
ADDRESS	ADDRESS
PHONE	PHONE

NAME	NAME
ADDRESS	ADDRESS
PHONE	PHONE

NAME	NAME
ADDRESS	ADDRESS
PHONE	PHONE

NAME	NAME
ADDRESS	ADDRESS
PHONE	PHONE

NAME	NAME
ADDRESS	ADDRESS
PHONE	PHONE

NAME	NAME
ADDRESS	ADDRESS
PHONE	PHONE

NAME	NAME
ADDRESS	ADDRESS
PHONE	PHONE

NAME	NAME
ADDRESS	ADDRESS
PHONE	PHONE

NAME	NAME
ADDRESS	ADDRESS
PHONE	PHONE

NAME	NAME
ADDRESS	ADDRESS
PHONE	PHONE

NAME	NAME
ADDRESS	ADDRESS
PHONE	PHONE

NAME	NAME
ADDRESS	ADDRESS
PHONE	PHONE

NAME	NAME
ADDRESS	ADDRESS
PHONE	PHONE

NAME	NAME
ADDRESS	ADDRESS
PHONE	PHONE

NAME

ADDRESS

PHONE

L'ANDALOUSE, MOTHER-OF-PEARL
AND SILVER (detail)
James McNeill Whistler
c. 1894
75⅜ x 35⅜ in.
Harris Wittemore Collection

NAME	NAME
ADDRESS	ADDRESS
PHONE	PHONE

NAME	NAME
ADDRESS	ADDRESS
PHONE	PHONE

NAME	NAME
ADDRESS	ADDRESS
PHONE	PHONE

NAME	NAME
ADDRESS	ADDRESS
PHONE	PHONE

NAME

ADDRESS

PHONE

NAME

ADDRESS

PHONE

NAME

ADDRESS

PHONE

NAME

ADDRESS

PHONE

NAME

ADDRESS

PHONE

NAME

ADDRESS

PHONE

NAME

ADDRESS

PHONE

NAME

ADDRESS

PHONE

NAME	NAME
ADDRESS	ADDRESS
PHONE	PHONE
NAME	NAME
ADDRESS	ADDRESS
PHONE	PHONE
NAME	NAME
ADDRESS	ADDRESS
PHONE	PHONE
NAME	NAME
ADDRESS	ADDRESS
PHONE	PHONE

NAME

ADDRESS

PHONE

NAME

ADDRESS

PHONE

NAME

ADDRESS

PHONE

NAME

ADDRESS

PHONE

NAME

ADDRESS

PHONE

NAME

ADDRESS

PHONE

NAME

ADDRESS

PHONE

L'ANDALOUSE, MOTHER-OF-PEARL
AND SILVER (detail)
James McNeill Whistler
c. 1894
75⅜ x 35⅜ in.
Harris Wittemore Collection

S

S

NAME

ADDRESS

PHONE

NAME

ADDRESS

PHONE

NAME

ADDRESS

PHONE

NAME

ADDRESS

PHONE

NAME

ADDRESS

PHONE

NAME

ADDRESS

PHONE

CAPTAIN SAMUEL CHANDLER (det.)
Winthrop Chandler
c. 1780
54⅞ x 47⅞ in.
Gift of Edgar William and Bernice
Chrysler Garbisch

NAME

ADDRESS

PHONE

NAME	NAME
ADDRESS	ADDRESS
PHONE	PHONE
NAME	NAME
ADDRESS	ADDRESS
PHONE	PHONE
NAME	NAME
ADDRESS	ADDRESS
PHONE	PHONE
NAME	NAME
ADDRESS	ADDRESS
PHONE	PHONE

NAME	NAME
ADDRESS	ADDRESS
PHONE	PHONE

NAME	NAME
ADDRESS	ADDRESS
PHONE	PHONE

NAME	NAME
ADDRESS	ADDRESS
PHONE	PHONE

NAME	NAME
ADDRESS	ADDRESS
PHONE	PHONE

NAME

ADDRESS

PHONE

NAME

ADDRESS

PHONE

NAME

ADDRESS

PHONE

NAME

ADDRESS

PHONE

NAME

ADDRESS

PHONE

NAME

ADDRESS

PHONE

NAME

ADDRESS

PHONE

NAME

ADDRESS

PHONE

NAME	NAME
ADDRESS	ADDRESS
PHONE	PHONE
NAME	NAME
ADDRESS	ADDRESS
PHONE	PHONE
NAME	NAME
ADDRESS	ADDRESS
PHONE	PHONE
NAME	NAME
ADDRESS	ADDRESS
PHONE	PHONE

NAME	NAME
ADDRESS	ADDRESS
PHONE	PHONE

NAME	NAME
ADDRESS	ADDRESS
PHONE	PHONE

NAME	NAME
ADDRESS	ADDRESS
PHONE	PHONE

NAME	NAME
ADDRESS	ADDRESS
PHONE	PHONE

NAME	NAME
ADDRESS	ADDRESS
PHONE	PHONE

NAME	NAME
ADDRESS	ADDRESS
PHONE	PHONE

NAME	NAME
ADDRESS	ADDRESS
PHONE	PHONE

NAME	NAME
ADDRESS	ADDRESS
PHONE	PHONE

NAME

ADDRESS

PHONE

NAME

ADDRESS

PHONE

NAME

ADDRESS

PHONE

NAME

ADDRESS

PHONE

NAME

ADDRESS

PHONE

NAME

ADDRESS

PHONE

NAME

ADDRESS

PHONE

MORNING IN THE TROPICS (detail)
Frederic Edwin Church
1877
54⅜ x 84⅛ in.
Gift of the Avalon Foundation

T

T

NAME

ADDRESS

PHONE

NAME

ADDRESS

PHONE

NAME

ADDRESS

PHONE

NAME

ADDRESS

PHONE

NAME

ADDRESS

PHONE

NAME

ADDRESS

PHONE

RIGHT AND LEFT (detail)
Winslow Homer
1909
28¼ x 48⅜ in.
Gift of the Avalon Foundation

NAME

ADDRESS

PHONE

NAME _____

ADDRESS _____

_____

_____

PHONE _____

NAME _____

ADDRESS _____

_____

_____

PHONE _____

NAME _____

ADDRESS _____

_____

_____

PHONE _____

NAME _____

ADDRESS _____

_____

_____

PHONE _____

NAME _____

ADDRESS _____

_____

_____

PHONE _____

NAME _____

ADDRESS _____

_____

_____

PHONE _____

NAME _____

ADDRESS _____

_____

_____

PHONE _____

NAME _____

ADDRESS _____

_____

_____

PHONE _____

NAME

ADDRESS

PHONE

NAME

ADDRESS

PHONE

NAME

ADDRESS

PHONE

NAME

ADDRESS

PHONE

NAME

ADDRESS

PHONE

NAME

ADDRESS

PHONE

NAME

ADDRESS

PHONE

NAME

ADDRESS

PHONE

NAME	NAME
ADDRESS	ADDRESS
PHONE	PHONE
NAME	NAME
ADDRESS	ADDRESS
PHONE	PHONE
NAME	NAME
ADDRESS	ADDRESS
PHONE	PHONE
NAME	NAME
ADDRESS	ADDRESS
PHONE	PHONE

NAME	NAME
ADDRESS	ADDRESS
PHONE	PHONE

NAME	NAME
ADDRESS	ADDRESS
PHONE	PHONE

NAME	NAME
ADDRESS	ADDRESS
PHONE	PHONE

NAME	NAME
ADDRESS	ADDRESS
PHONE	PHONE

NAME

ADDRESS

PHONE

NAME

ADDRESS

PHONE

NAME

ADDRESS

PHONE

NAME

ADDRESS

PHONE

NAME

ADDRESS

PHONE

NAME

ADDRESS

PHONE

NAME

ADDRESS

PHONE

NAME

ADDRESS

PHONE

NAME _____

NAME _____

ADDRESS _____

ADDRESS _____

_____

_____

_____

_____

PHONE _____

PHONE _____

NAME _____

NAME _____

ADDRESS _____

ADDRESS _____

_____

_____

_____

_____

PHONE _____

PHONE _____

NAME _____

NAME _____

ADDRESS _____

ADDRESS _____

_____

_____

_____

_____

PHONE _____

PHONE _____

NAME _____

NAME _____

ADDRESS _____

ADDRESS _____

_____

_____

_____

_____

PHONE _____

PHONE _____

NAME

ADDRESS

PHONE

NAME

ADDRESS

PHONE

NAME

ADDRESS

PHONE

NAME

ADDRESS

PHONE

NAME

ADDRESS

PHONE

NAME

ADDRESS

PHONE

NAME

ADDRESS

PHONE

THE CAT (detail)
Unknown American Artist
c. 1840
16 x 20 in.
Gift of Edgar William and Bernice
Chrysler Garbisch

UV

UV

NAME _____

ADDRESS _____

_____

_____

PHONE _____

NAME _____

ADDRESS _____

_____

_____

PHONE _____

NAME _____

ADDRESS _____

_____

_____

PHONE _____

NAME _____

ADDRESS _____

_____

_____

PHONE _____

NAME _____

ADDRESS _____

_____

_____

PHONE _____

CHELSEA WHARF: GREY AND SILVER
James McNeill Whistler
c. 1875
24¼ x 18⅛ in.
National Gallery of Art, Washington
Widener Collection

NAME _____

ADDRESS _____

_____

_____

PHONE _____

NAME

ADDRESS

PHONE

NAME

ADDRESS

PHONE

NAME

ADDRESS

PHONE

NAME

ADDRESS

PHONE

NAME

ADDRESS

PHONE

NAME

ADDRESS

PHONE

NAME

ADDRESS

PHONE

NAME

ADDRESS

PHONE

NAME	NAME
ADDRESS	ADDRESS
PHONE	PHONE

NAME	NAME
ADDRESS	ADDRESS
PHONE	PHONE

NAME	NAME
ADDRESS	ADDRESS
PHONE	PHONE

NAME	NAME
ADDRESS	ADDRESS
PHONE	PHONE

NAME	NAME
ADDRESS	ADDRESS
PHONE	PHONE
NAME	NAME
ADDRESS	ADDRESS
PHONE	PHONE
NAME	NAME
ADDRESS	ADDRESS
PHONE	PHONE
NAME	NAME
ADDRESS	ADDRESS
PHONE	PHONE

NAME	NAME
ADDRESS	ADDRESS
PHONE	PHONE

NAME	NAME
ADDRESS	ADDRESS
PHONE	PHONE

NAME	NAME
ADDRESS	ADDRESS
PHONE	PHONE

NAME	NAME
ADDRESS	ADDRESS
PHONE	PHONE

NAME	NAME
ADDRESS	ADDRESS
PHONE	PHONE
NAME	NAME
ADDRESS	ADDRESS
PHONE	PHONE
NAME	NAME
ADDRESS	ADDRESS
PHONE	PHONE
NAME	NAME
ADDRESS	ADDRESS
PHONE	PHONE

NAME	NAME
ADDRESS	ADDRESS
PHONE	PHONE

NAME	NAME
ADDRESS	ADDRESS
PHONE	PHONE

NAME	NAME
ADDRESS	ADDRESS
PHONE	PHONE

NAME	NAME
ADDRESS	ADDRESS
PHONE	PHONE

NAME

ADDRESS

PHONE

NAME

ADDRESS

PHONE

NAME

ADDRESS

PHONE

NAME

ADDRESS

PHONE

NAME

ADDRESS

PHONE

NAME

ADDRESS

PHONE

NAME

ADDRESS

PHONE

UNDER FULL SAIL (detail)
Unknown American Artist
Second quarter of the 19th century
26 x 20¾ in.
Gift of Edgar William and Bernice
Chrysler Garbisch

W

W

NAME

ADDRESS

PHONE

NAME

ADDRESS

PHONE

NAME

ADDRESS

PHONE

NAME

ADDRESS

PHONE

NAME

ADDRESS

PHONE

NAME

ADDRESS

PHONE

FLAX SCUTCHING BEE (detail)
Linton Park
1885
31¼ x 50¼ in.
Gift of Edgar William and Bernice
Chrysler Garbisch

NAME

ADDRESS

PHONE

NAME	NAME
ADDRESS	ADDRESS
PHONE	PHONE

NAME	NAME
ADDRESS	ADDRESS
PHONE	PHONE

NAME	NAME
ADDRESS	ADDRESS
PHONE	PHONE

NAME	NAME
ADDRESS	ADDRESS
PHONE	PHONE

NAME	NAME
ADDRESS	ADDRESS
PHONE	PHONE

NAME	NAME
ADDRESS	ADDRESS
PHONE	PHONE

NAME	NAME
ADDRESS	ADDRESS
PHONE	PHONE

NAME	NAME
ADDRESS	ADDRESS
PHONE	PHONE

NAME

ADDRESS

PHONE

NAME

ADDRESS

PHONE

NAME

ADDRESS

PHONE

NAME

ADDRESS

PHONE

NAME

ADDRESS

PHONE

NAME

ADDRESS

PHONE

NAME

ADDRESS

PHONE

NAME

ADDRESS

PHONE

NAME	NAME
ADDRESS	ADDRESS
PHONE	PHONE

NAME	NAME
ADDRESS	ADDRESS
PHONE	PHONE

NAME	NAME
ADDRESS	ADDRESS
PHONE	PHONE

NAME	NAME
ADDRESS	ADDRESS
PHONE	PHONE

NAME _____

ADDRESS _____

_____

_____

PHONE _____

NAME _____

ADDRESS _____

_____

_____

PHONE _____

NAME _____

ADDRESS _____

_____

_____

PHONE _____

NAME _____

ADDRESS _____

_____

_____

PHONE _____

NAME _____

ADDRESS _____

_____

_____

PHONE _____

NAME _____

ADDRESS _____

_____

_____

PHONE _____

NAME _____

ADDRESS _____

_____

_____

PHONE _____

NAME _____

ADDRESS _____

_____

_____

PHONE _____

NAME	NAME
ADDRESS	ADDRESS
PHONE	PHONE

NAME	NAME
ADDRESS	ADDRESS
PHONE	PHONE

NAME	NAME
ADDRESS	ADDRESS
PHONE	PHONE

NAME	NAME
ADDRESS	ADDRESS
PHONE	PHONE

NAME _____

ADDRESS _____

_____

_____

PHONE _____

NAME _____

ADDRESS _____

_____

_____

PHONE _____

NAME _____

ADDRESS _____

_____

_____

PHONE _____

NAME _____

ADDRESS _____

_____

_____

PHONE _____

NAME _____

ADDRESS _____

_____

_____

PHONE _____

NAME _____

ADDRESS _____

_____

_____

PHONE _____

NAME _____

ADDRESS _____

_____

_____

PHONE _____

DR. PHILOMEN TRACY (detail)
Unknown American Artist
c. 1780
31⅛ x 28⅞ in.
Gift of Edgar William and Bernice
Chrysler Garbisch

XYZ

NAME

ADDRESS

PHONE

NAME

ADDRESS

PHONE

NAME

ADDRESS

PHONE

NAME

ADDRESS

PHONE

NAME

ADDRESS

PHONE

NAME

ADDRESS

PHONE

THE SKATER (PORTRAIT OF WILLIAM GRANT) (detail)
Gilbert Stuart
1782
96⅝ x 58⅛
Andrew W. Mellon Collection

NAME

ADDRESS

PHONE

NAME

ADDRESS

PHONE

NAME

ADDRESS

PHONE

NAME

ADDRESS

PHONE

NAME

ADDRESS

PHONE

NAME

ADDRESS

PHONE

NAME

ADDRESS

PHONE

NAME

ADDRESS

PHONE

NAME

ADDRESS

PHONE

NAME	NAME
ADDRESS	ADDRESS
PHONE	PHONE

NAME	NAME
ADDRESS	ADDRESS
PHONE	PHONE

NAME	NAME
ADDRESS	ADDRESS
PHONE	PHONE

NAME	NAME
ADDRESS	ADDRESS
PHONE	PHONE

NAME

ADDRESS

PHONE

NAME

ADDRESS

PHONE

NAME

ADDRESS

PHONE

NAME

ADDRESS

PHONE

NAME

ADDRESS

PHONE

NAME

ADDRESS

PHONE

NAME

ADDRESS

PHONE

NAME

ADDRESS

PHONE

NAME	NAME
ADDRESS	ADDRESS
PHONE	PHONE

NAME	NAME
ADDRESS	ADDRESS
PHONE	PHONE

NAME	NAME
ADDRESS	ADDRESS
PHONE	PHONE

NAME	NAME
ADDRESS	ADDRESS
PHONE	PHONE

NAME	NAME
ADDRESS	ADDRESS
PHONE	PHONE

NAME	NAME
ADDRESS	ADDRESS
PHONE	PHONE

NAME	NAME
ADDRESS	ADDRESS
PHONE	PHONE

NAME	NAME
ADDRESS	ADDRESS
PHONE	PHONE

NAME

ADDRESS

PHONE

NAME

ADDRESS

PHONE

NAME

ADDRESS

PHONE

NAME

ADDRESS

PHONE

NAME

ADDRESS

PHONE

NAME

ADDRESS

PHONE

NAME

ADDRESS

PHONE

NAME

ADDRESS

PHONE

NAME	NAME
ADDRESS	ADDRESS
PHONE	PHONE

NAME	NAME
ADDRESS	ADDRESS
PHONE	PHONE

NAME	NAME
ADDRESS	ADDRESS
PHONE	PHONE

NAME	NAME
ADDRESS	ADDRESS
PHONE	PHONE